Battle Scarred
new and selected poems

Jason L. Ammerman

Battle Scarred
new and selected poems

Chatter House Press
7915 S Emerson Ave, Ste B303
Indianapolis, IN 46237

chatterhousepress.com

Library of Congress Control Number: 2012944411

ISBN: 978-1-937793-06-7

CONTENTS

Forward

Scars. Some are visible. Some are not. Some might cause embarrassment either by where the scar is, how it may look, or even by what caused it. Some scars are even worn as a badge of honor. But regardless, they all have a story. This book is a testament of scars. Scars of faith, family, friendship, integrity, love and humor. All things that create human triumph and tragedy. Although that type of scar is not physical, they often can take on a life of their own. A life of frivolity, debauchery, lechery, loneliness, unreasonableness, or depression. Finding mindful balance in a minefield is survivalism. That is the battle. Pain is the teacher. Life is suffering. What doesn't kill makes you a poet.

Poetry. No other craft is older. Still, no other craft can deftly maneuver through good and bad encapsulating the essence of the moment. Sometimes when there are no words to say the unsayable, a poem is forged. Nobody does this better than Jason L. Ammerman. On the page or stage this spoken word artist will grab you by the heart and the throat simultaneously. Wake you up and shake you down. Give you a glimpse into your insides, parts busted up and bleeding--all the while giving you a gentler hug into his catharsis as reaffirmation that you can get through anything. Like he has. Because
we all have our own war stories to defy.

If hope is a medic a poem is medicine. After all, a scar is a mark of healing. At times we all need a little healing, right?

Matthew D Jackson
AD 29 January 2012

BATTLE SCARRED

BE

This is where it's happening

Man/too many cars manage
To speed through this intersection

Honking

Quoting ancient laments
From the books of Yusef and Kerouac
The Psalms of David

The streetlights hiss
The neighborhood theater
Acts out

Performances

By the poets
To stand and ride for
To kill and die for
To bleed themselves for

On this corner
On that corner

Today/everything is holy

This is where it's happening

This is where Jesus will come back
To toss craps to win His robe back
To destroy the rusted spear
To wave it in the air
To proclaim this land in the name of His Daddy

This is where the Atheists come with their paddy wagon
To throw Jesus in and the keys away

To give Jesus a beating
To deny His teachings
To deny what we are standing for

On feet that are falling apart at the souls

Where the Atheists exalt the name of Achilles
To tattoo black tears underneath eyelids

But this is where it's happening

We stand for what is believed in
And we take this back to the intersection
Speaking metaphors that will
Bring the summer to love you
And the spring to hate you in the same breaths

To teach the Double Dutch kids
Using nursery rhymes as a basis
To study a thesaurus
To write poems on the sidewalk in neon chalk

Must be the devil
That keeps muting Baraka
Back in the intersection
Must be the devil
That forgets the names
Of Dunbar and Whitman

Must be the love
That keeps calling Ms. Giovanni
From her domicile
Causing her to go late on rent
Rather than to miss out on
All of this creativity

Must be the love
That allows for the ghost of Tupac
To water the weeds that force a

Blossom out of concrete cracks
Into the forms of roses
This is holy

This is our scene and all we get is a name

Poet
As if it were dirty
Whispered from behind a bar of soap
Making us hate to go to bed at night
Making us dread the existence of school superintendents
And real estate clauses that make sense to only lawyers

Poet
We are poets
As the voices become faces
Mocking the government from afar
Hiding from behind the bell of a musical instrument
Taking the compliment of beautiful language

Belittling it into that of reasoning behind
Getting high and leaving it in the back of the mind
Waiting for the moment where one can stand proud
Without their knees buckling
Without their sweat pooling into their palms
Skipping the meat for a little rest and realization

That this is where it's happening

Poet
Just a poet
Just a crack in the side of a condemned building
Just scratches down the backs of pushers and addicts
Who dot the landscapes with their views of
You ain't nothin'

But a poet
Taking a backseat to the rest of the arts
Red headed

Ripped into parts of flesh of His flesh
Blood of His blood
Ashes to ashes and dust to dust

Tossed into the empty pen
Of the rabid reminders of fads and consequences
Trained by blonde hooker pop stars
Owned by reality television
Syndicated by gloomy November mornings
Ashes to ashes and dust to dust

Because Che just didn't do enough walking
For this world to grasp what he was trying to say
About the dangers of growing up in a world
Of babysitter LCD TV picture boxes
This is their world soon to be our world once more
This is our world no more their world

Poet
We are poets
And this is where it's happening/poet
This intersection/poet
Be proud of it/poet
Just be/poet/just be

Tuning in California

A wrinkle in time
The hands on the face of my watch
Mocking
Crowded with visions of Ginsberg holies

Pure geek fun and god-unlike godheads
Beatnik/nearer to incorporated townships
To thee/I bequeath this old pair of leathered
Gloves/they are drivers or they were drivers

Nineteen sixty-seven

We were touring the world
The heights of mountainous veneer smiles
Pure white like the numbers on the radio dial
I can still feel my fingers tremble as I reach to

Find Soweto on the frequency modulated conversation
I was a little hurt up front but I was personal
Because you have to be broken
Because it was a drag/was a drag/was a drag

The blue ink love notes
Written in chicken scratch
The finest ever
Offered from a chicken who was wasted

On easy-riding onion skin biographies
Tuning in California from the back of a VW
Painted up to represent the latest trip never taken
With egg men and walruses among other Beatles references

Some life in nineteen sixty-seven

Poetry in motion/her mother called her that
Poetry in motion/her mother despised that
Poetry in motion/what I wanted to desperately leave alone

But she would only let me call her Ruth

Pure geek fun and god-unlike godheads
Beatnik/nearer to incorporated townships
To thee/I bequeath this old pair of leathered
Gloves/they are drivers or they were drivers

Nineteen sixty-seven

I have written a love song for Soweto
Ruth
See/I have written it with you in mind
I started writing and this is what came out

Give love a chance
Dig love in advance
Before you know what
Or who is beguiling you

Picture yourself leaning back
Into your favorite easy chair

Picture me sitting across from you
Reading your favorite novel out loud

With my best faux British accent
For one day I will be your man

Or I will still be wooing you from afar
Behind that shady elm tree
Dreaming of wedding cake
Ripping away the head of the groom
With my rotting teeth

Give love a chance
Dig love in advance
Before you know what
Or who is beguiling you

8

How I used to dream of piercing your ears
Washing away the make up from last night

How I used to dream of comforting you
With the idea of a ghost who follows you

Around your living room as you dust family pictures
And I will be right there to fill them
With photographs of nineteen sixty-seven

With smiles and gazes that are all the rage in Paris
Around lunchtime/where I loved you
Hiding within the stanza of a poem

A love song for Soweto
Ruth
See/I have written this with you in mind

Going back west
Where peace is appreciated
With your sundress and long blond hair
Your pirouette features

Where feeling Indiana would be the
Center of our conversation for our parents
If they were still alive and kicking

Like the old albums
The ice in the pictures
Is as beautiful as the velvet upholstered loveseat
That old eyesore of Midwest apartment fixtures

I think I can see your face in the ice
With a look of determination
That can only come with finding Soweto
In the words of a love song

This ballad for Ruth and her paperclip clan
Office political revolutionary

It's gonna be alright
Tip of the hat to John Lennon and whether
Or not you dig Yoko/all you need is love
A ballad for Ruth and her paperclip clan
Office political revolutionary
It's gonna be alright
Just flipping them toward the door
That leads into the Vice President corner office

The wall/decorated with flabbergasted faces
Memories of brainstormy seas
Think tank and I know it sounds insane
Especially with your long hair and hatred for drugs

Ruth
I have heard news from the front lines

Berkeley has outlawed the United States

Looking at my watch
I am on time for a change
Just a boy
Spilling Tyrannosaurus Rex bones
All across the patient linoleum
As I sing Ring Around the Rosie
In a stolen pair of sneakers

You used to tell me
That the kids are not the same
As they were when we were coming up
Saturday Morning cartoon feel-good murder

You used to tell me
That I am not a reflection of the recent heroes
Their bows and quivers are just accessories
To dance with/to bag chicks with
And I know it sounds insane
But you should expel the long hair
And still hate the drugs

For more of a routine way of
Falling in love

I remember why I miss you
Ruth
I am all the way back in Indiana town
So far away from tuning in California

A love song for Soweto
Ruth
See/I have written this with you in mind
And I don't have any idea how to end it
So I will end it this way

Story of a City

Here's a little something funky
To get your feet tappin'

Hell hounds on the trail
No one plays
Around here/we always sleep late

Past the hiss of the streetlights
Standing sentinel
Their gaunt frames
Fading into obscurity
No one cares for them

Not like the starless sky cares

We substitute
Their protection with bling
With shiny things
Akin to broadside accidents

To the beat
Ya don't stop
Get down on it
Breakdance

Flop like a fish
Gathering a last breath

The project walls are emergent prison cells
Chalk drawings on cinder block walls

Kilroy was here!

Kilroy was late
Like a welfare check

Our kids like ice cream

From the mobile corner store

Showing off souls
Through the window
Nailed shut to save energy by a super
Who wants to get a tax cut by not
Using as much heat as the body needs
To make love on a Saturday night (Sinner!)

Using grimaces to show how it feels good
When the touch of a fingertip on a hidden piece of flesh
Is enough to stand up
To rejoice in the Name of a God
Promising eternal life

If we have our way
We will be remembered long after we die

Outside/there's a manhole cover over the hole
That we've dug for ourselves in the wake of
Cold breezes spoken through hip hop lyrics
Expelling the words out of high school
Out into an atmosphere to challenge satellites

How they go round the outside/round the outside
How they go round the outside/round the outside
The satellites go round the outside

Like the needle rests its laurels on wax
Like the neighborhood kids spell their names in the snow
Like a love song is no more than

Taking a bow
Placing it atop a box
Vibrating the future
With rhyme
With deejay licks
With lollipops hanging from lips
Like existing dangerous

Like being famous
Like repenting sins
Just to get back in the game
Like Michael Vick
Volunteering at the dog pound
In the gas chamber

One aim
Two stones
Put two and two together and
You get four score and
We hate math so we don't care
How long ago it was when we arrived
At that fork in the road
Where we chose the path of least resistance
Where we chose the side of the most selfishness
Where we lost our faith and still make claims
To know God like the backs of our hands
Where we still manage to thank God
For getting paid millions knowing that
The first dollar came from a drug sale
Where we hide our worry by committing drive-bys
With our lights on for someone is always home
In that house
Right over there
Boarded up windows

I remember watching PBS children's programming
Cross legged on that floor
I remember my grandmother
Giving me cereal at the kitchen table
I remember the cockroaches as they
Scattered at the flick of the switch
I remember the sheriff's sale
That stole my childhood
Replaced it with a funeral after
Ninety-One years of life

She always loved me

Never treated me badly
Even when she didn't know my name
Who I was as I stood next to her bed
Her death rattles overcoming
I was overcome

I keep this inside
My head
As I take a bow
Place it atop a box

Merry Christmas
Happy Birthday
Have a good Arbor Day
Happy Valentine's Day

For my wife
I cannot compose a good enough love poem
To reflect how the feelings got in the way of
Being bad to the bone by taking the bone
And slipping it inside of her lady parts

Yet
There is a legacy that is left
Melting away the meddle
That forced me to flash devil signs
As a young teenager with raging hormones
Sitting in his room
Smoking weed
Cigarettes
Alternating them accordingly
Famously living out
What the songs dictated to me

I watched it on TV
As the Senators grilled my idols
Over their lyrical choice
Blaming a suicide on Ozzy and Priest

Nowadays
I walk with a virus in my head
Making me sick until I spit up blood
Onto pages and pages recollections
Disguised as
Rehashed as
A story of a city

Molded into fables of
The ones that got away
To be traded in for
One who stayed
And how I love her
Unconditionally
Undone

They say that children are the future
They say that our surnames will carry on
Like the neighborhood

When I look into the mirror
I realize that my opinions
Are muted by the privilege
Of becoming a father
I shut my mouth up

I've made this so many lines
But I gave seven to Vietnam
In the name of my father
Who fought another man's war
Over there
They sent them there
Over there
Only to return to a world of confusion
To a world of disrespect

Nowadays
I walk with a virus in my head
Making me sick until I spit up blood

Onto pages and pages of recollections
Disguised as
Rehashed as
A story of a city

Molded into fables of
The ones that got away
To be traded in for
One who stayed
And how I love her
Unconditionally
Undone

I lie in bed
Covered up to my neck
I am afraid of ghosts
Stealing my safety blanket
Stealing my protection

What I have to say is this

Take stock in your relationships
Keep them close to your breast
To listen to your heartbeat

So many hollow eyes
Walk through this life
Their choices made
When life is tougher
Than the leather that was worn
As an adolescent
Trying to make sense out of a life
That continues to breathe life into you
Regardless of your lungs being so full
That you suffocate on the same air
That defines you and your freedom
To exist in the Name of God
Just like you defy anyone
Who tells you that you can't

Nowadays
I walk with a virus in my head
Making me sick until I spit blood up
Onto pages and pages of recollections
Disguised as
Rehashed as
A story of a city

To remind me of where I came from
To remember the history
To state the words rubbing the bleach
From the bones that hold my posture

Slavery
One demerit for the class for participating
Shackles
Traded in steel for bling
Shame
Hanging the head until someone rubs the nape of the neck
Surprise
That new pair of shoes for the eight year old
Made by another eight year old

Sanity
Existing in a circular room and told to stand in the corner
So
The answer to many questions posed by the people
Slander
Guarantees to get the highest office in the world
Solution
Revolution
Solution
Revolution

Straight from the Americanized Dictionary of Congressional
Understanding
I pledge allegiance
To know my own strength
As I stand out here in the rain

Letting it wash away the dirt
As it catches my chest
Glistening
Because I still have a need to feel good about myself
My body
As I stand in front of the mirror
Mentioned before
Overplayed
Like a bass bump
Race card
Hidden up the sleeve
Of the neighbor
Where his job is in danger
Of being sent overseas
To save a few bucks
On labor

We have run out of luck
It seems
Our arms wrapped with barbed wire
To remind us
That the government doesn't need a fence
To keep us in
To remind us
That spending our lives repenting
Doesn't mean that we need to answer for their sins

I pledge allegiance
To nothing short of God
In a world of oxymoronic truths

Politics
What we do is for the benefit of us
Passion
What we feel is for the benefit of us
Psychology
What we tell you is for your benefit
Prayer
Thou shalt have no other God before the flag

Pink
Living for a charity is better than putting food on your table
Perversity
It happens in all cultures (See Rome)
Punk
Usurpers will not be tolerated
Preference
Votes count except in legislation

Funeral for a Friend

The car won't start again
Think it's just being stubborn
The female neighbors are wearing their shorts again

And I am black garbed for the funeral of a friend

Poncho and Lefty on the radio
Willie Nelson always puts me in a good mood

His voice reminding me of my bandito past
My fedora hiding in my closet even to this day

I'm not too old to know that, once, we laughed at
The more silly things that make life worth living
Like cemeteries and late night horror flicks
Where the ghoulish host called us by name
As he eyeballed his sub sandwich just off camera

I'm not too young to realize that immortality
Is just a figment of our upbringing
The hymns sung in church on Sunday mornings
Taught us that we can only go so long
Before our kindness makes us explode into the cosmos

The car won't start again
Think it's just being stubborn
God is hanging out in the apartment
Pacing and disappointed

Oklahoma doesn't seem so far away
When someone asks me if I know Jesus

And I am black garbed for the funeral for a friend

In the rear view mirror
I am white haired and wrinkled
As I curse my vehicle

For not wanting to say good-bye

I'm not too tired to explain my troubled times
To an open ear at a random bar in Indianapolis
The drinks, stiff and cheap and leaving me with broken bones
Reminding me of my younger days
As I fantasize about the better days

I'm not too ignorant to know that sacred words
Are more than just mere Bible verses
Exorcising the devil out of my daily struggle
Sprinkling my childhood generously with sugar
Culling my bicycle out of its coma

I pick up the newspaper/headline reads:
In the know about a policeman who retired
Without a single kill/without a single arrest

And I am black garbed for the funeral of a friend

The keys jingling/annoyingly/from the ignition
Houston/we have a problem
Think it's just being stubborn

My wife is rolling her eyes
I am in love with her more than ever today
My hands are reaching for her comfortable assurance

As I say farewell
Knowing that I don't have to be there
In person
Incognito
Behind shades
No sun up in the sky today

Just the memories
Reaching down to tap me on the shoulders
They're still around

Like God
Jesus
Like the seasons change
Like funerals are supposed to be solemn events
Like the dead are still hanging around
Watching the whole damn thing going down
Like farewell

Waylon Jennings

Sometimes
We need to get back to the basics
Where any reference
To the Hatfields and the McCoys
In song
Deserves a pedestal to stand upon
For society to recognize
Keeping up with the George Joneses
With no more than a cowboy hat
And a drinking problem
So yes
Let's go to Luckenbach, Texas
Where we can have a drink
Where everybody will be feelin' no pain

Willie Nelson

That's all
Just Willie
Needn't say more than that name
It comes packed with a joint
And rebel yells all around
Until we get thrown out of town
Then we'll be on the road again

Small Town

Coming in/the box cars are coming in succession
Three cars in/a child/licking his wounds/stigmatic
Five cars past/a police officer builds a fortress out of hope
Eight cars/the switchman shines the light guiding in a war

It has taken centuries to reinforce this dream
Out of Rocky-style Underdog excitement
All of the men file out of the factory on the edge of town
Spinning their tires/launching dirt and gravel into the atmosphere
And their women/oh/the women cook and clean and birth babies
Like old school chauvinism shackling them to purity
Like ice cream cones dug out of frigid chasms

The circus is coming to town for this independence celebration
Paul Klee inspired/going crazy from this heat/angels rise to face
The devils that close off this town from modernism/bobby socks
Soda pop and black and white television/husbands and wives sleep
In separate beds/no teenage pregnancy/no miracles on ice/no need
For Disney movies to remind them that life is all about whistling
While they work/grease monkey/southern drawl promising that...

Coming in/the box cars are coming in succession
Ten cars in/the preacher is hiding his secrets under his jacket
Eleven cars/the basketball star signs his name in blood to be a first
rounder
The final car/the final solution/something wicked this way comes

No rain ready to wash away the aches and pains of age
Only the realization that death comes in threes/sixes and if sixes were
nines
Death would come at 27/at the bottom of a bottle
With aspirations to be the next rock star to sell out thirty years after his
demise
How irresistible/to be a misfit/to be touted at the next big thing
Even after one has become the next big thing in cremation
Not even the bones of inspiration left after it is all over

This celebration is for those who live awestruck/their eyes
Lulled back into a middle school innocence full of crushes
Full of bad choices not learned from/full of good spouse handbooks
A ball of light in the northern sky/falling fast/across the main street
Beneath the street lamps/a man in black sits/smoking a cigar
His fingers boney/his smile rigid but with reason/he is waiting
He is waiting/he is waiting…not for you…but your soul…

The box cars stop right in front of the train depot
Filing out of the cars/freaks and animals/all turning over a new leaf
To let it float in a bucket of dreams/this middle American standoff
Where Jesus slept here/where real men know Jesus…

The women/oh/the women begin to quilt the town's history
Into the fabric that makes them who they are/voting party lines
Forming to the right/golden promises weighing down conversation
Bubbles/falling upon empty heads/knocking out idealistic contemplation
That somewhere out there/is a big city/with big city realities
A sneaked kiss in the park next to the fountain where two lovers met
yesterday
And the day before/all doing the same thing as this couple today

Makes me want to come home/where I long to embrace rock and roll
Sniff hyacinth/I am a fake/with my plague doctor's mask/with my
Wax vampire teeth/with my cynicism born of old boy's Hollywood
Yacht sailing/rape/where the movie star walks away unscathed
Until the media embellished his story like his belly/fatty/we are all fatties
With our secrecy/with our papal conviction/no/I don't lie as much as you
Think I lie/but I lie nonetheless/makes me want to come home … to be
free

Rain

You're not so beautiful that I should come in out of the rain
You're not so beautiful that I should come in out of the rain
You're not so beautiful that I am not so stupid that
You're not so beautiful that I am not so stupid that
You're not so beautiful that I should come in out of the rain

But I could use an umbrella

All of the windows in the apartment building
Have faces looking out at me
From behind red brick
As if any other color would bring out other distractions

All of the tenants in the apartment building
Have faces looking out at me
From behind political soapboxes
As if an abortion story could bring out the sympathy in me
I am sorry

But I could use an umbrella

You're not so beautiful that I should come in out of the rain
You're not so beautiful that I should come in out of the rain
You're not so beautiful that I am not so stupid that
You're not so beautiful that I am not so stupid that
You're not so beautiful that I should come in out of the rain

But I could use an umbrella

The trash collectors are out in full force today
Collecting neglected children
Out of rat infested homes
As if their bones rattled with each crack-pipe inhalation

I heard a story about a narcotics detective
Breakdown
I am sobbing in my own puddles of tears

Wishing for a world
Of Asimov realities
Shaking up my bronchi
I don't want to breathe

But I could use an umbrella

You're not so beautiful that I should come in out of the rain
You're not so beautiful that I should come in out of the rain
You're not so beautiful that I am not so stupid that
You're not so beautiful that I am not so stupid that
You're not so beautiful that I should come in out of the rain

But I could use an umbrella

Dodging family pets
Leaping from the eaves in mass suicide protest
Of dog parks
Their gods looking down in approval
Etching a new rule
Into the Book of Bark
Commandment 11: It's okay to bite the hand that feeds

Can I borrow your slicker, Rock Star?

For no one will loan me an umbrella
For I am brave enough to stand here in the rain
To proclaim my love/for all things are perfect
Like our lives/a cup of coffee in the morning
Like a poem written in vain
Knowing that no one will care to read it
Wadded up but unafraid of being found

I could use an umbrella

Gaza Strip Oom Bow Wow

Gaza strip oom bow wow
My mama told me as she
Glided her stares to meet
The news television screen

They fight like dogs
She told me
With their cap guns and
4th of July rockets that go boom
Inside of small restaurants

She told me of Malibu
The patron saint of sunburst terrorists
Skin cancers amass beneath the dermal attempts
To assassinate the eagle

A young boy quakes the sands of Tel Aviv
Die for Allah!
Live for Allah!
Echoes of martyrdom squeak past the censors
Who long to be surfing

Gaza strip oom bow wow
Like all Jewish love affairs
Are born with crucifixes in hand
With gray hairs on their heads
My mama told me
Are seeds for a new and improved racism

Meanwhile
Back in this old corner of Indianapolis
U.S.A.
There is a crippled reflection
Of special effects British slums

Gaza strip oom bow wow
And I've never blown up a Muslim
And I would never blow up a Muslim
Even if Jews believed in Christ

Gaza strip oom bow wow
My mama told me
That the pretty little bomb in the window
Is really a pretty little child
Pulling down the blinds to hide
From the bomb choo-cha bomb bomb

I can run a mile and a half
If I can outrun a bullet

Meanwhile
Back in this corner of Indianapolis
U.S.A.
Elvis Presley is advertising free love
With a shimmy of his hips
A shake and a kiss
A hunk of burnin' love
Endorsed by a war on drugs
Banned by the ghost of Ed Sullivan
Waist down
Deep in Saudi crude

Gaza strip oom bow wow
Modeling like a show girl
Her lips
Taste sweet
Like olives

I long to touch her
My eyes
Conquistador excitement

This is an American poem

Reincarnation
99 times born Mohammed
Tracing heritage back to a Jewish root
The movie star centuries of pre-fab hanging gardens
As oasis

Gaza strip oom bow wow
My mama told me
As I swallowed alcohol aristocracy
Created art out of intense origami
Folding passions into plainly sculpted causes
As I detonate my four limbs to the four corners

My heart lands safely
In Marion County
Indiana
U.S.A.
Pep and vigor
August 13
Today is a good day to be a martyr
In memory of the twin towers
NYC
WTC
9/11
That was a good day
To smother innocence
As Bush tackles economy at forum
Air travel remains an industry in turmoil
This is an American poem

As love has found us
Gave us breath
We live by the carry of the eagle
Over land and sea

Gaza strip oom bow wow
My brother told me

As he dug passages of biblical parables
Quoting Jesus
For word as it appears on currency in Latin
My frustration is wrapped in black satin

Gaza strip oom bow wow
Where I hang my hat
And cuddle with oil well infernos
Where I sleep soundly
This is where God has unbound me
A fish
Walking bass up and down Chi-town scales

As love has found us
Gave us breath
Held our heads when we were
Deep in debt

Our castle status is as tattered
As the sari worn by Gandhi
Blood stained from assassination

As we embrace the false light
Surrounded by sweet St. Babylon

We flex our arms
As we are tempered
With the promise of divine sex
With wives
Hidden behind the veils of chauvinism

Son
This is an American poem

Son
Gaza strip oom bow wow

What it is
IS
Just what it is

We live by the carry of the eagle
Over land and sea

We live by the mercy of God

Nineteen Seventy-Three

I slipped on banana peels to come into this world
My tongue continues to speak of revolution
In a dialect forgotten about over centuries of European expansion
Forgotten about during slave trades
Forgotten about on Columbus Day festivities

My mother scattered her values over my crib
Letting them land upon each of my fingertips
To weave a world of peace and I want it now

My mother placed a language on my forehead
In the form of a cross made from the ashes of
A past/of a man who sacrificed everything for me to be

As a child/I skipped math class and went straight to history
Writing out the truth that there were great socialists
Hidden among the racists of a two-party system
Giving birth to the sadists of a 21st century political machine
Where Strom Thurmond is considered a hero
Question mark that sentence for I am confused
Like a modern art masterpiece
My head restricted to that of a thinker

My finger pointed at the front lines of a war
Enlisting privatized swat snipers
Hidden like the candy in a piñata too beautiful to break

They file in/the students/scholars of what is right now
Tired and poor and we have more right to be here
Than the one per centers/ninety-nine percent can't be wrong
Question mark that sentence for I am confused
Like the value of Pi
My gift is that of a life
That can easily be misconstrued as a poem

A flower growing/I am the proof
That there is something bigger than a missile

Or a six-figure salary or a broken beer bottle
Over the head of an alcoholic who swears
That one should never bring a gun to a knife fight

I slipped on banana peels to come into this world
And I am still landing on my feet
An Open Letter to Cable TV

Top one reason that I won't watch your damned show anymore:

I am in love with my wife
She is in love with me
We have better things to do late at night

Robert Johnson

I went down to the record store
Fell down on my knees
I went down to the record store
Fell down on my knees

Paid $25 to experience genius
'Nuff said

Elvis Presley

Most people bawl him out
Thief!
Catfish eatin' Mississippi boy
Rhythm and blues
Swagger on stage
Pre-diabetic condition forcing a clown
Out of movie stardom
Dying too young
Before him time
Rock and roll never forgets
Innovation
Rock and roll never forgets
Passion
Rock and roll never forgets
To remind us that it all began somewhere
For us white kids anyway

Heaven

An old rusted out Chevy pick up
In an old almost abandoned drive in

Tonight
The old west seems to be bigger than life

Over oily French fries and watered down sodas
She reaches over to hold my hand/a slight smile
Stretches across her soft cheeks/my weathered face

This is where we will remain forever
In mind
In heart
Even if we are locked up in cages
Forced to give information about our loved ones
Our country
God bless the U.S.A.
Red
White
Blue
Blooded middle class truck driving young folks
In love on a Friday night at the drive-in

Freedom (on the Roadside)

rubber tread
mouth watering
singles' lines rehearsed
he had never tasted freedom
until that night

the dirt on his hands
caked
into his callouses
roughhewn
that night

he was the savior
reflecting the moonlight
off of his lapels
a Bible in his pocket
a gift from the Gideons

in that one motel
stuffed into the nightstand
next to his insecurities
of being a loyal lover
to her on the roadside

he had never tasted freedom
until that night
her touch
soft like silk
over bleached bone

his gaunt body
beneath that three piece
a bow tie that practically choked
him
senseless

his gibberish speech
made for good humor
over
coffee too strong
to be called coffee

but
its black center
allowed for such a name
like
a first impression is usually wrong

about her
her body
perfect
pre-fab sculpted
in this desolate America

they made love
beneath the wide eyed moon
of their ancestors
this ecstasy of conestoga wagons
go west

young man
go west to meet the evil
that comes east
to aim his six shooter
to recite his favorite psalm

he had never tasted freedom
until that night
as it rested upon his tongue
her future waited
for his decision

to fall in love with her
as she sits Indian style
in crabgrass

letting the chiggers sup
on her imperfection

but
in his eyes
she is perfect
she is past
she is present

she is the future
tall skyscrapers
money laundering schemes
she is the promise of
political tornadoes

she is
late for her musical expertise
she is
he is
a seventh day mandala

he is
nothing
his kiss
means nothing
an apocalypse of sex

she is
radical
she is
he is
an Atlantic tempest

he is
psychology
his fears
are founded
an art to his madness

he had never tasted freedom
until that night
over campfires
roasted dreams of being successful
of being more than just a soul

that dances amid the flames
as they rise to greet the same
creation that had birthed
the both of them
at the moment of big bangs

hand claps from God
a supremacy
written across papyrus rolls
saved for millennia
a love supreme

he is blissful
when they are finished
their loving
their touching
their reeling in the road

she is wondering
where this will take her
she is not thinking about him
as much as he is thinking about her
he is in love

she is not
she is a distraction
she is a lunacy
lacking brevity
her poetry is maddening

he is
she is
a story to tell

he is
the failed hero

she is
racked with guilt
for she wants to care
but this roadside
will not let her

before they were lovers
he was
an icon of hobos
she was
a princess of passion

rubber tread
mouths watered
singles' lines rehearsed
he had never tasted freedom
until that night

Stranger

Give me a truth
An angel with blue eyes entered on invitation
A passion felt with such strength
To choke on butterflies

Jack, Jim, Jason & John

Houses blowing up out in the country, tonight
Police are running overtime to protect and serve
Shiny badges and rubber bullets with names on them
Like the days of World War Two bombing runs, tonight

I am laughing and pointing fingers like there is no
Tomorrow, we will be meeting up for a couple for the road
Over reminiscing, over 70s light rock love songs
Over what's-her-name from high school, tonight

She is watching a romantic comedy on cable
Her husband is down at the tavern and he's caught
On the losing side of an addiction, maybe he'll
Come to his senses before the last call, tonight

Jack is cooking up dinner for a crowd of kin
Pot roast, mashed potatoes, and they're dancing,
For there is nothing in the world that means more
Than family, face to face, arm in arm, they pray, tonight

Jim is risking his strong shoulders by carrying loads
For nameless teenagers and football game fixes, for
College meant more to him than just the beginning of a career
It meant something like throwing up his arms in prayer, tonight

Jason is writing his blood onto onion skinned paper
Rolled out like compassion for just another Christlike figure
Dressed in furs and jewels and promises of bigger and better
Politics for the meek and their earth that reaches up to pull them back,
tonight

John is watching his mother as she sleeps
So peaceful that she is even keeled, even in the throes
Of geriatric tailspins, one day becomes a month becomes a year
Becomes a robbery of a valued embrace on a Sunday morning, tonight

She is watching a romantic comedy on cable

46

Her husband is up in Heaven waiting for her
Over tea and dessert and God, why does it have to be this way?
Coming to her senses, she is ready to go, tonight

I am a story for telling; tee time, labeled and golden golf clubs
Pulled to shoot that little dimpled ball into the atmosphere
To meet the moon with a heartfelt handshake, the trial will be
Televised for all those who give a damn about the past, tonight

Houses being rebuilt out of calloused hands for those less
Fortunate for their lives lived and their deaths dealt, for their
Futures and their histories and their church bells tolled to call
Them in, face to face, arm in arm, they pray

Superman

A wooden door/windows hazy/glossed over
For the real funnies/pasted to privatize the comfort
Of changing clothes inside of a telephone booth

Saving the day
Without the wisdom
To save the world
Before a disaster happens

Blue pantyhose/red capes and millions of kids
Idolizing forever/holy/in his actions/makes his
Chest hurt to know that she is crazy now

That she waits for him
Inside of a Hollywood ranch
Two car garage
A bullet in the gun

They say his ghost is still there/lying in wait
Weightless/as he rampages through the room
Looking for a love letter that never was mailed

Always watching
Cannot stop a war
Cannot lock the door
Cannot recognize these new faces

So he leaps tall buildings in a single bound
More powerful than a locomotive
But he can't stop a speeding bullet

Saving the day
Without the wisdom
To save the world
Before a disaster happens

Fixing Cars

Jeremy is under the hood again
With Derrick, Jimmy and A.J.
And all of their friends
Drinking and talking about the latest trends
And I don't know nothing about fixing cars

They try to explain to me
What a fuel injector is
But I don't know nothing about fixing cars

They try to break down the math
In how combustion begins
But I don't know nothing about fixing cars

If I knew 20 years ago
That to change a battery
I'd need a friend
I would've learned a lot about fixing cars

It seems that they're speaking Greek to me
All that muscle car talk
And
Dreamy eyed gazing at a wheel rim

But I know poetry and they ask me
To write love poems
So they can give them to their girlfriends

I know how much it costs
To run my car through a car wash
I know who to call when I need a new wiper blade
But I don't see the relevance of knowing the difference
Between a 454 and a Hemi
Therefore I know nothing about fixing cars

Jeremy is under the hood again
With Derrick, Jimmy and A.J.

And all of their friends
Drinking and talking about the latest trends
And I don't know nothing about fixing cars

I don't know nothing about fixing cars

Meeting the Family

He caught his shirtsleeve in the car door
Pulling it apart at the seams and it seems
That he is more nervous than they are

His mindset is Paris in the summer of 1970
So far away from the war back home
He is a dancer/a people watcher/a poetic politician

Rhyming his anti-Vietnam rhetoric
No Gooks to kill over in this budding metropolis
He blames his lack of people skills on falling in love

He caught his shirtsleeve in the car door
Gently tugging as to not attract attention
From Aunt Gertie with the obviously fake teeth

He is infantile
Curling up on the porch
Just outside of the front door

He is into her right now
Slipping a song lyric
Neatly into the palm of her hand

He'll be careful not to hurt her
In the face of fire and brimstone Christianity
Tearing down rock and roll busts of ancient Caesars

He caught his shirtsleeve in the car door
That is where all of this began
Flash forward to now where beautiful cousins appear

To rescue him with a bottle of whiskey
His heartbreak is not for a lack of attention paid
He remembers his youth

In school/where all of the good children got fudge

At the end of a long day of recess and grammar lessons
And football lesions left of who's better/who's best

Breaking down sentences of criminal activities in conversation
No Gooks to kill over in this budding metropolis
He thanks his Daddy for cleaning up and finding Jesus

He caught his shirtsleeve in the car door
Shaking his free fist at the skies to tempt God
Into coming by for a cup of tea or a game of chess

Birthday

Imagine your mother's eyes
Upon that first fresh breath of hospital air
Hypnotized by stretching arms and legs
Infatuated by a world full of knowledge

But the doctor needs to cut the cord first

Imagine your father's pride
As you take your first steps in their living room
Against a backdrop of news reports
Fuzzy stories on oil embargoes and stock market slumps

But the doctor needs to cut the cord first

You will be an athlete
A young man of the first line
College grad
Attorney for the rich and famous
A heart
Giant and alabaster
Like the kings who came before
A chip off of the old block at the core

But the doctor needs to cut the cord first

Imagine an afternoon of barbecues and patriotism
To awaken the next morning to airplanes
Turned into missiles and people throwing themselves
From windows to keep from dying long term

Where you will dream of faraway lands
A gun in hand
You will be a soldier
It is not laid out in front of you

Happy Birthday!

Bonsai

The tree's reflection in my computer screen
How it moves
Like a harmonic guitar solo

I don't mind the cockroaches
As they scurry
Across the hardwood
With good sportsmanship

My head lulls back
As if to anticipate the rapture

Incoming
A star crossed rise to fame
The bonsai and the Christ
Sharing time
With my breathing

In and out
Of my trunk
Of a chest

My olio of emotion
Turning the frown upside down
Smiling

A black and blue
Bruised ego

My palms are sweaty
Nerves
Comfortable outbreak of acne

These thrifty years of existence
I want to be a samurai

My armor rusting through

A message
That
No one will take seriously

As
Long
As
I drive this red sports car
Through this midlife crisis

And that damned tree
In my computer screen

I contemplate a logical move
To stop writing about reality

I tell myself
To be dominant
One must seize
The ice cream cone
From the child
Forcing a cry from
His/her mouth

Must edit that out right now

The guy from downstairs
Is throwing his trash out

We got guys on the street
Killing themselves
Over one twenty dollar bill
At a time
Over one three line stanza
At a time

I have finally become bored
With reality television
I have finally become bored

With "this is what you get"
Radiohead references

But if you are willing to wait long enough
This poem will become interesting

Reality Television Lament

We sing out loud
Off key
In the shower
In the car
In private
In church ... HALLELUJAH!!
Next to other parishioners who can't sing
Their tongues flipping in the summer breeze
As the opening credits begin to roll

The star is the husband cheating on his wife
With the beatnik waitress at the local coffeehouse
Dominated by old men practicing Zen meditation
By masturbating underneath the tablecloth with one hand
Sipping stale black coffee with the other

But on the television...

We watch arguments
Openly
Six feet under
Six foot tall
With fists flying
After dipping themselves in lye
To burn the skins off of their competitors
And how easy it was
To meticulously place our personal ads
Into the rinse cycle
For the cameras want us
Yes/they want us to call them
When we decide to have sex

To appear on the mother of all shows
Called Pangaea
Pulling together different continents
They have to live together ... Amen!
HALLELUJAH!

Preacher/we ask that you pray for us
We ask that you mix it up
The music
The acting
The rhetoric
The temptation
The inability to change the channel

Our demons are nervous
Anorexic
Bulimic
Bipolar schizophrenic getting high
At the club
Making a path for their first victim
Hogging the camera for a minute or two

The only thing that can save us
A power outage

Bobby Kennedy

As you were bent
    Knees creaking with anticipation
    For a change
Discussing the future of the United States
    With a child
A grain of rice dancing the tango through her fingers

As you were crouched
    Heart beating
Sunshine peering through the clouds

I remember my last night at the drive-in
Coveting the chick in the next car
Making out in the backseat
With the high school football quarterback star

It was that moment
Where I realized how lonely of a planet
This is/where we live
I'm dying/crying

I'm mad as hell
Was mad as hell
But your words saved my life
That night

Quoting poets
Sending anti-riot messages
Lamenting
The death of your peer

Our sights were blurred
Our aims were a little off

The crosshairs of your speak
Were slightly misconstrued
But you understood/rich white boy

Embracing the black man's struggle

We wanted to be sedated but wouldn't be able
To admit that for another ten years
From beneath the streets of NYC
Punk rock and if you would've lived

You would've known

Our hands
    Wrapped in the fluidity of fire
Our sicknesses
    Left to warm on the back burner

Of a government
Dead man
Dead man
Dead man/my brain is set to twitch
From the thought that this would've been
Something awfully rehabilitating

    Had
    Your
    Speech
    Not
    Included
    Indianapolis

What went down in history as a moment
Serves to be a calling card for us know
To stand and puff out our chests
To grunt
To raise fists
To decry this war

As you were crouched
    Heart beating
        Still alive
            Still alive

Karaoke Bar

His bass drags down his performance
Bitter beer face

He doesn't care whether anyone does
Or does not enjoy it

This rite of passage
Beats the hell out of playing air guitar
In his parents' basement

Hate

If there was one thing that unsolicited advice has brought me
Hate
Drum beater/the skins of your anger
Sound like a hundred years of genocidal rock and roll
Beat me dead/out of me/out of my system
I wanna scream/I wanna thrash my filthy skin
With tattoos depicting tragedy
Forgotten saviors
Do me a favor ...

Hate me

If there are people out there who get under my skin/I've learned
Hate
Politician/the laughter of your promises
Shatter my eardrums with a decibel out of control
Rock and roll me/out of me/out of my system
I wanna vote/I wanna give up my freedoms
With submissions signed openly
X marks the spot
I don't have a lot to lose ... so

Hate me

I want to stare down/from my ivory tower
I want to stare down/from my ivory tower
I want to crumble cities/with my index finger
I want to sing melodically/with my hatred throat
I want to stare down/from my ivory tower
I want to stare down
I want to stare down

Too many finger pointers/hooker's daughter
Promising unconditional love/slamming the
Front door when she gets high and sneaks
Out to meet the girlfriend/luna/tidal/moves me to ...

Hate me

If there is a moment where I feel a little less than I did an hour ago
Hate
Veiny wing harpy/the cull of your song
Rips away my ribcage forcing me to starve
My faceless me/out of me/out of my system
I wanna love/I wanna go back to 1969
With four on the floor grinding
Blood pools
I don't know my name anymore/stereotype me

Hate me

Too many rubberneckers/sexless marriages
Massacring unconditional love/rotting the
Teeth out when she tires of kissing me and leaves
Me with a t-shirt wrapped around my jaw/crunch hard ... to

Hate me

I want to stare down/from my ivory tower
I want to stare down/from my ivory tower
I want to crumble cities/with my index finger
I want to sing melodically/with my hatred throat

Pigeon Fight

The two poets are tired of discussing poetry
Tired of rehashing memories of John Dillinger
It smells like soap and shoe polish out here

A heavy sigh escapes the more talented of the two
As he launches a heaping spoonful of Chinese food
Each grain of rice/limply/failing at flying
Only to end up enjoying a movie star's death
Sounds like the business end of a panty raid out here

The flapping feathered wings of scavengers
Everyone is gathering around
A short homeless man holds up a quarter
Begins to take bids on the winner
The great white hope

The two poets are tired of discussing poetry
Tired of falling in love with the rhythm method of memorization
Their stomachs turn in anticipation of a bloodbath

The pigeon is the scabbed remains of a scuttled culture
The pigeon is the underdog of the cancer of urban sprawl
The pigeon is holed up and waiting for the bell to ring

The two poets are tired of discussing poetry
Tired of debating the importance of pop music
Versus pop culture versus pop rocks and soda

As the secretary from the skyscraper a block up
A block over/she turns away in horror
As the pecking commences/oh/the humanity!

The lesser of the two poets dives into the crowd
Attempting to find Godot for he knows that he is here
The pigeons can take all of this away

The poets are here

The poets are tired
A homeless man holds up a quarter in lieu of a cigarette

The two poets are tired of discussing poetry
Tired of grinding guitars and all night titty bars
Smells like soap and shoe polish out here

The two poets are in the mood for a fight

God is in the Desert

He is always twenty or thirty clicks away
Dancing His fluid prophecies out
There is something going on
Outside of what is at hand

Nothing is what it seems

Last night/there was a cold rain
Intoxicating as love/made me long for home
Dreaming of love in three-part poems
This is what is at hand

My prayers recited loud and clear
From the cannons that litter the landscape
The tattered flags that tattle on us
The remnants of Aramaic persecution curses

We are not so far from where Christ was born
Crucified
Left to die
Earthquakes and Easter eggs are music to American ears

He is always twenty or thirty clicks away
His living Word/existent among the Shepherd community

At night/they dance
Praise Him in a childlike awe

They tell us that He is bigger than all of this inbred fighting

When I see Him
I always get a sense of home
What it is supposed to be
More like Rockwell
Than Cain and Abel

The Shepherds tell us that God knows

That God knows when something has gone horribly wrong

Tonight/I pray
Loud and clear
I pray for my child
I will return
To tell her of
Finding God in the desert

Different Drums

We march to different drums
Self-inflated egos
Mama's boys
Gone off to save the world
One live round at a time

Yesterday
We went into a village
They still live in mastabas
Shepherds by day
Conspiracies to murder us by night
Roadside

Their children come up to us
Wanting a piece of our uniforms
Some chocolates

We give them guitars
For the truest American gift
Is rock and roll

We teach them to dance to Elvis
To shimmy their hips

Today
I am writing you to tell you
How strange it is to inspire children
Who will grow up to
Not hate us

It is strange how our talk of God gets us
Closer to Him in an empty desert
Than any church could

We know He lives
Here
Where no one can bug Him

With trivial prayers for a job promotion
A new red sports car

The only red out here
Is the Blood
That Pastor Charlie speaks
Passionately
It is Easter

We are just neighbors here

Mom
You would've laughed at these kids
Trying to sing Elvis songs as if their hearts
Had been ripped away from their chests
By the same love that keeps me missing home

I wonder if I could've experienced this
If I had joined the Peace Corps

But we are keeping the peace

I know what you're thinking
How proud you are of me
Saving the world from terrorism
It is just what I imagined it to be
A few skirmishes here and there
But for the most part
Pretty boring
Hot

By the way
I got your care package
Thanks for the baseball cards
Now
I can reminisce about my childhood
How innocent we were back then
Going on patrol
Listen to the drums

Abandoned Smokestack

We save our pride for days like this
The sun rising
Prayers to be recited
As we fill the line to get out

We are completely silent
Just short of the occasional smoker's hack
Cancer taking root
Yet/playing second fiddle to what is happening

Right now

We will insert our timecards
One last time
Head over to the bar
For a last round

We are completely silent
Just short of the occasional smoker's hack
Light up another
Let the past be swept away

That was ten years ago

Just yesterday
The sun was rising
Prayers being recited
As we dove underneath the hood

That old '67 Chevy
We were completely silent
Just short of the occasional smoker's hack
Hanging in the air like a ghost

We have a deadline of next Saturday night
Sam and Dave on the radio
We're tapping our feet

Think to ourselves about nostalgia

About the last round
Before everyone moved out of town
We are completely silent
Just short of the occasional smoker's hack

Light up the old smokestack
Remember the past
That was swept away like the dust
Of a hard day's work

Let it be swept away

Doc

Inside this chair/leather molding around my mind
In my mind/I'm a disco-dancer/auto-checked/open up and
Say…Ahhh! /Reminds me of those old days where
Low flying planes had something to say/buzzing by
Our ears/I can't hear you/what'd you say? /I SAID!!!

All of our chickens have come home to roost in grey
But blue in the faces/it has been 150 years since we
Fired that first shot/sucker punched/just because I'm
Missing some teeth doesn't mean that I'm missing
Some teeth/all lions lose their machismo at some point

A man cannot believe in himself when those around him
Resign to hold him down/tie him down/torture him
Waterboard him/drown him/yet/I'm reminded of something
My father told me/you're only old when you regrets outweigh
Your dreams/and man/I ain't finished dreaming yet …

So Doc/stick your tongue depressor down my throat
Listen closely/that cavernous refrain you are hearing …
Ahhh! /should remind you that sunlight is reserved for
Special people and man/you haven't earned enough
Rolls of pennies to be able to convince me that I'm gonna die …

Mickey Mouse Role Call

She stood outside on the platform/bags packed/her name ...

Just another Susie
Just another engine boiling stinking motorbreath
      In the distance/we can hear thousands of fans
      Chanting one syllable names/fists pumping
Just another Susie with eyes on making it in the big city

They stood outside on the platform/nervous tics hanging on
To ticket stubs/a slight bounce to their standing/sentient/letting
The music overtake their souls/melding with veins/blue blooded
Rich kids/gold sold for a way out/for another life/for vampires

Just another dozen
Just another Friday night beer-induced bar fight
      The crowd gathers in the wings/to dance spry
      Like children of Icarus/only the sun can bring them back
Just another dozen dimly lit stars

But she is not just another star/she is who the stars look up to
For her determination is stronger than the freight trains that
Push their way in and out of town/east and west/like the neon
Signs that read, "Only the rabid shall survive!" rather than ...

    Jesus Saves/tattooed to their arms
    Like one-way tickets to the next world
    Their names upon arrival/etched into the Book of Life
    Lambskin bound by ravenous stares of old pioneers
    Lost in the Rocky Mountains/by the gaunt reminder
    Of children starving to death in the deserts of Africa
    By the blistered souls of South American children
    Traded for religious rites/we are all stars here but ...

She is the one/the promise/the sleeping tiger/the American dream

Wordsmiths and Professional Sports Athletes

I have about 20 minutes to get into gear/play me some of those old
Motown records
So I can sit and grin/shaking to get off the pot/laughing out loud/saying
nothing just ...

Writing a poem in my head to slam dunk hard/shattering glass
backboards/to get paid
Thousands of dollars for weekends/we all live for the weekends/to grow
ten feet tall

I have about 20 minutes to get into gear/conga line forms to the
right/limbo/to the left
How low can we go? /spiking the punch/punching the spiky-haired
hipster/this is ours

The show/the stage/the mic/the solid proof that we have earned this
30something dialogue
Script from the teevee show that is long forgotten/but still just as
boring/limbo/to the left

My politics is about as sensible as rock and roll/wouldn't wanna live that
way but it
Sure gets my feet to tapping/head to nodding/veins to pumping/so why
do I love this?

Because it's mine just like this street/these needles crushed underneath
my feet/this alley
These homeless vagrants squatting/it's all mine/the verse/the religion/the
music ...

I have about 20 minutes to get into gear/play me some of those old
Motown records
So I can reclaim my ego/puff my chest up/spar with my cohorts over who
is best in ...

This town/where the funeral pyres are as shiny as the gold lining the
gutters/two men

Enter/one man leaves/Bartertown is not just a movie set/a poem is not just a prop

A crutch to lean on/it is a lifeline/a straight line drive into center field/an 82-yard touchdown
Pass unmolested by a lockout/because it is mine/it is perfection down to the lips ...

Pouty/with attitude/sexual frustration/empty promises/long train rides/disappointment
Like a doctor's office/morose/with a silver lining when Billy Joel comes on ...

Clean Bill of Health

And with a shake of the hand/twist of the wrist/I am thrown back into my
mind
The reality of good jokes/being chased by a gaggle of geese in
nature/mean little
Bastards of glory/their medals decorating their breasts/white like
expensive real estate

I want to plant my flag there/tonight/like being stoned/tossing pills down
the toilet
To coax a good piano solo out of a tired song/a stiff drink and we're all
here ...
Even Glenn Miller's ghost/which explains the whirring in my ears/the
space between them

As festive as a carnival/side show barkers/come see the beast with more
than one head
Two arms/a leg and a half/oddity/hunchbacked/history laden with images
of frontier
Medicine men promising a clean bill of health with one swallow of foul
tasting elixir

Next year/I'm gonna build me a house/change my name to Uncle
Sam/wear red/white
And blue/hang a flag from my porch every day of the year/embrace
patriotism like
A hammer and scythe on a red background/fist raised/and aching back
from loads carried

Like a good little employee/150 years ago/we fired the first
shot/today/we are paying
To watch our livelihoods stolen from us/150 years ago/we were doe
eyed/prancing through
The forests/free like the beginning of time/like God promised us/like we
feel when we vote

Pulling the lever/and with a shake of the hand/twist of the wrist/I am
realistic these days

We don't get younger/but we are just right/today/my name is Sonoma Cabernet/1973
Today/the only thing that escapes me/is/when my next doctor appointment is ...

Back in Black (The Throat Culture Menagerie)

Back in black/fifteen centuries have passed since those words were etched
Into our veins/blood pumping guitar rocking sons of bitches/back in black

I'm back in black/remembering those who came before/King David and his psalms
Dante and his hellish dreams/Ginsburg and his drug-induced supermarket trips

So I'm back in black/garbed for the funeral of a friend/Dateline: Dayton, Ohio
April/2011/spoken from the grave/one foot hanging out/balance out of whack

Teetering somewhere between summer and fall/baked beans and grilled hot dogs
Ants crawling over our bare feet/we are the universe for some species/somewhere

We are the gods/dogs of war/our breastplates riddled with Illinois bullet holes
Stained with the history of persecution/round worlds and a silent God whose

Long face and sunken eyes tell the story of His children/where somewhere
Deadhead bumper stickers became fashionable/fast forward to today ...

Back in black/rocking out to sunshine/flowers/nudity done in a tasteful way
How quick we are to mourn where we began/fearful of where we are going

The future seems a little out of reach when all we have is right now to sit back
To enjoy the show at hand/and now ... ladies and gentlemen ... open up and say, Ahhh!!

Passing Notes

Gregorian chants echo
This sterile environment of cubicles
Charts
Numbers
Dollar signs

All of the end signs are here
Six hundred and sixty-six accounts
All of them

This mutated method of checks and balances
Board meetings
Bored meetings of men and women over cocktails
These thoughts fleeting
Feeding off of leftover carcasses of contracts signed

Murder is just another thought to pass the time
Until lunch dates in fine restaurants
Where the secretary looks as appetizing
As the snake is tempting

Forty days and forty nights
In front of a computer screen
Connected
Brain to phone receiver
Where a note is slipped into her fingertips
In between the f and g keys on the keyboard

Dear you,

Next to the water cooler
Your phone number waits
Amid the answers to all of your questions
New age
Where crystals call you names
As you whisper my name
Extra sensory

My perception of you is that of a dog
Looking for a bone
I can hear you
Centuries away
I love you
Want to make you love me

Sincerely,
Me

Love Is

Built out of a foundation youthful indiscretions
Baited out of history lessons to be learned from

Love is the sum of all prayers thrown out into
An atmosphere/where words carry themselves
Like upstanding citizens/all of the smart kids
Wear glasses/they can see the future disguised
As monstrosities/skyscraper buildings/the truth
Set free to lay waste to a world devoid of atrophy
Hold yourself in that bed and count your sheep

Love is the reminder that we all fail at the same
Tasks that designed the pyramids/ancient languages
Languish to spite logic/we are not as devoted as
We claim to be/angels fly above us and we cry
Terrorists/so much has changed since ninety-nine
Prince songs don't allow us to dance anymore
Because our pants hang too low/Praise Jesus!

Love is the grey area between black and white
Relations/black socks irritate my white feet
But that doesn't make me wanna go out and lynch
White coconut makes me cringe when I think of
Eating it but that doesn't make me wanna go out
And who are we to dictate what is right/what is wrong
What is this love thing?/we need to figure it out soon

Love is the end of the world as we know it
The modern theft of music and overlaying tracks
To complement our verses/we wage war by
Saying that we are too powerful to be overtaken
When we are overcome by the lyrics of a song
We weep as we bid adieu to our loved ones
Our heartbeats are the chisels carving out a home

Love is the rock that hides beneath our feet
Stepping left/right/cross over/right/left

Skipping the conversation for the main course
Of meat/taking the leftovers to make an outfit
Out of bone/the smell alone would be enough
To drag us off into deep R.E.M./where the
Gun bought for protection would be as useful as

I love you like a sniper is perched on a knoll to change the world
I love you like a prize fighter's dizzying final moments

Love is highlighted amongst the clouds
As they dump gallons of rain upon our heads
Documented by beautiful and smart meteorologists
But there is a flood of secrecy in their eyes
As they unwrap their souls before the camera
Adding ten pounds of Christian resurrection
To the belly of the beast

I love you like the sun setting over the horizon
I love you like the right versus wrong argument that plagues my mind

Love is you and I on a Saturday night
Love is you and I meeting in a hallway
Love is you and I sharing a drink
Love is you and I making promises to keep them
Love is you and I making a baby out of real love
Love is you and I giving giant metal sevens to Vietnam

The Name Game

Just the look in your eyes
Beneath the sheet of a parka
Pouring rain

We belong in an old Hollywood romance

How you breathe around me
Leaves me stretching my fingers
Out to feel the honesty of your name

Your name is green
Fields of waving long grass
The edge of the briar is teasing us
Culling us alive
To kick our feet up
To the Good Lord's Heaven
Where Saints and children sing choral arrangements

My name is wind
Picking up the memories that lay
Along the side of a dirt road
To save
Inside the glove compartment
Of a car on blocks
Rusted and beautiful

We think about all of the broken hearts
Left of a world
To be replaced by
Bigger and better walls
Brick
Red
Like the blood that courses through

Our name is free
Fluid
To awaken each day

To forget the sun
To forget the moon
To start anew
To fall in love again

For it is the journey that
Gives us a reason to live
To forget about the clichés
To stand independent
Of loneliness
They say that today is our day
To live forever

To express love
Through the information that is slipped
From index finger
To thumb
To index finger
To thumb
To lean in for a kiss

A General Poem

I like my chicken
Fired up
And
Angry
For losing its head

No chicken should trade its head in
To be a number on a menu

Darwin

Uptight
My spine cracks under the pressure
Of being handed another cigarette

I take a drag
I am cool like the other monkeys

Celebrity

She's got dirty hair and she's alone
She's got dirty hair and she's alone
She's got dirty hair and she's alone
She's got dirty hair and she's ... sssshh ... we don't talk about this
                    Around the dinner table
                    Snubbed for wine and small conversation
                    About schooldays and how the meat has a
                 Wonderful spiciness to it/the war on the TV screen
           The war/Joey/down the street/star wrestler/got called up/served
        His country/he didn't make it back/friendly fire/they call it/we don't talk
     About it around her/she is sad/she hasn't showered in weeks/she hasn't gotten out
Of bed in weeks/this is her life in the fast lane/this is her classic rock song to sing along wit

The Cars are on the radio again
She says that they are so lame

She wants to write a paperback novel
She would like to name the main character something extraordinary
November

Imagine the creases in the cover
From being read so much as if
Hidden within its pages was a lifelong love affair
Where earrings are hidden between pages 22 and 23
Where stockings are held down by a tattered mattress
Full of bedbugs and used to pay the bills

She wants to write a paperback novel
She would like to set it somewhere boring
Indiana

She smokes and drinks to live the life of a writer
No more a poet than Dylan Thomas on his last shot
Slumped over the table like a Hugo character
Her finest moments spent with Joey
Her finest moments spent with Joey's memory

She wants to write a paperback novel
She wants it to be better than other novels
Other novels suck

Joey left her because it sounds good in a novel
He doesn't pay child support because he is dead
And that makes him a little more dangerous
Than tomato soup and grilled cheese served
On a platter to her on a November Sunday afternoon
She still doesn't like the Cars and never will

She wants to write a paperback novel
Exhausting all other means of getting over Joey
She wants to live

She's got dirty hair and she's alone
She's got dirty hair and she's alone
She's got dirty hair and she's … sssshh … she's alright for a while

It seems that all of her days begin like this

She doesn't cry anymore
She has no reason to cry anymore

There is no spilled milk

She uses the backdoor
All of her friends are out of jail
Pawning off their jewelry
To throw off the anger of buying blood diamonds

She remembers her first brush with love
Flower power and Joey
Knee deep in protest
A beauty and her feminine wiles
Trapped beneath her and her feistiness

She's got dirty hair and she's alone
She's got dirty hair and she's alone
She's got dirty hair and she's … sssshh … she wants to live forever
She's starting to wonder what death is going
To be like/gripping her chest in fear that this may be
The big one like some old 70's black exploitation movie/she
Is blue/she is tired of being alone/she is tired of living with her choices made
She is tired of her multiple choice answers opted for/she is tired of all work and no play
Makes for her to be a dull monkey/her spoon is bending benign/no Uri Geller explanation

She doesn't care
She doesn't care
Get her a cigarette
Howling
She is a werewolf
New to this loving herself thing
It's hairy
She doesn't care
Get her a limo
She doesn't care
Get her a drink
She is a writer
She is innocent
She doesn't care

Because she's eating better
She thinks that we should experience
Her
Forever

Thunderboomer

Tonight/I fall asleep/with a ghost next to me
Hollowed/I wait/for this ghost to love me back

I am watching the atmosphere fall like rain
From my window/where pain is more than a frame
To wrap around a picture taken on a special evening
A noose tightening to keep me from swallowing
This bitter pill that is the size of a nightmare storm
Swirling above our heads until the thunder shakes
Our faith from the bones out to the skin

Tonight/I dream about/telling the truth as it
Festers/like a rotten piece of meat/love me back

In the mirror/I am auditioning for the role of
A lifetime of rock ballads and whiskey history
Liver disease/blurry vision and a clutch play
Held inside my hand/my palms sweaty/my future
In question/fucked up off of speed metal and
Heroin lies/I wasn't as addicted to you as I was
Infatuated with my own failures of the skin

Tonight/I finger painted a scene from our past
Colorful/I pray/for this ghost to love me back

Sixties

Starting off with a bang/this is about my father
Affectionate and radiating unadulterated heroism
His actions bringing forth a new vision of the sixties

No more would the dinner table be
Decorative liquor bottles/their labels
Peeling off at the heat of my touch

No longer would my voice be a whisper
At the family reunions that dotted the
Landscape with dark secrets like blood

Lines drawn into the escape of persecution of
Unwanted pregnancies by mothers who
Are too powerful in their own right

He told me that she was the reason
He left/to join the Army/to make a name
For himself when his surname wasn't enough

His medals rattle the cardboard boxes littering
An ancient attic/and his mother didn't even tell him
About his older sister until he was back from Vietnam

And his father never got to tell him how much he loved him
On the eve of his inaugural sixties integration
My dad's grandfather never made it to his birthdays

Even those he shared with his twin brother/a hell raiser
Before the era of razors to cut out our pasts that
Come back to haunt us like ghostly chains rattling

And I never managed to discuss my worries about age
Just like I never understood the wake of destruction
That was left by failed marriages and alcoholism

Just like we never talk about the past unless it

Refers to insurance papers and what to do if he dies
This is the reality that the sixties has left me

I explain to my father how much free love bothers me
He looks at me/blank/his expression tells me everything
He hates hippies just like he hates terrorists

Just like he would save the life of a complete stranger
As if it were instinct, for his occupation was burned into his veins
So deep/that he wept on September 11 more than ever before

My dad is a dichotomy of blue collar revolutionary spirit
His frilled white sleeves are really a badge with a number
1065/molded to stand out before anything else; he is just a number

He owns several suits that line his closet
These flags of his brothers kept under lock and key
To present him with more than just funerary reminders

But he never ceases to amaze me
When he asks me for the keys to my vehicle
To run from point A to point B

Jason/he enquires/can you write a poem for a friend of
Mine? /this request/a resounding echo of 21st century bass bump
And grind in rush hour traffic/I ask him/who dies?

He is silent/his sixties almost over
He looks away/I begin to sift through his papers
This is the reality that the sixties has left me

Advice from a Father

Son
Don't give up on your dreams
Just make sure
You get paid well
When you cash them in

The Most Perfect Spider Web Ever Created

Today, I saw the most perfect spider web ever created
I ponder who is behind this spectacle of beauty

I think of Stephanie and her long lost song
Knowing somewhere/it's playing on the radio
Progressive Rock radio

While the sun forces us to higher ground
To hide from the dust as it gathers
Leaving a layer of resistance on family heirlooms

Handed down like lyrics/like pie at Grandma's house
I imagine a few background singers/lalalalalalalalala
Pray for the Big Man with the sax as he is embraced for the last time

Today, I saw the most perfect spider web ever created
I toast it with a frothy beverage and let my mind wander

Prayers are meant for those who are not functioning alcoholics
But I attempt it anyway/as if I were speaking to someone
Well-known/but not asking for an autograph out of respect

While the rains begin to come down/heavily/washing away
The faux wisdom that a grown man claims/his fame/his famine
Is the selfishness of politics and summer nights with a radio

Spread out/looking up to the stars/letting the bouquet of the
Freshly cleansed grass/throwing him back into childhood
Where he was safe/where three lines of poetry could heal

Today, I saw the most perfect spider web ever created
And I wanted to destroy it for what it's worth ... nothing

For these days/I have a low opinion of almost everything
Where I spin my media to include 180 degree turnarounds
Where death is just that … a way to repave the road of good intentions

Today, I saw the most perfect spider web ever created
Are you there, God? It's me …

Tattoo

Your voices lift to part the clouds
To carry angels on your words

Your love is that of innocence forgotten

Your purpose is righteousness

You're just as much a child of God
As I am a child of God
As we are saved

There is a tattoo on the arm
Etched into the skin

It is faith
Destined to be an instrument
To be the beautiful music played
To bring light to the shadows

There is a tattoo on the arm
Marked for Christ

Stumbling through days
Facing sin with a weapon in hand
This love for the Lord will be

Our personal demons gather
Stare at the body
The heart does not taste well
When the heart is full of unconditional love

Forgiveness breeds
Through the Blood
We all have the Blood in our veins

There is a tattoo on the arm
It is faith

For one should not live by one fish alone
For we were taught to fish for our entire family
For we will shatter the jars that hold the history
Of our faith hostage inside of them
For it should be known that we are marked for Christ

There is a tattoo on the arm
It is faith
Marked for Christ
Unbound

We Just Wanna Know

Sometimes
When we dream
Of the flowery stuff
That convinces us
We are kings

Sometimes
When we think
The world is made up
Of apple pie
Rock and roll make up
And cream

Sometimes
When we laugh
Out loud
Fracturing
Those faces that mock us

We realize
We aren't all that we are
Cracked up
To be

Rather chips off of old blocks
Grown up around'
Weeds
Dying to be
Where we thought we knew it all
Before

We realize
Our eyeballs are buried
Inside of Saturday morning
Bowls of cereal
Acting irresponsibly

We are the manufacturers of stories
Building muscles
Feeling the elasticity of the strands
Holding masterful maturity hostage

We point fingers
Pull levers
Our voices are hope
Our voices are change

The guard
With their rusted guns
Their potent drugs
Their relaxed promises
Of corn futures

Their money
Their sexual triage
Built out of love

And love is the thread
Forcing a binge out of
Safety in numbers

We watch
The corners
The spirits of cancerous actors
Dancing in our periphery

We brush the hair away
From our brow
Sweaty

Sometimes when we create
Our fingers heavy
With the paint
To tag brick walls with imaginary names

Sometimes when we flaunt

The gold
Stylish
That chokes us
From the wallet to the neck

Sometimes when we stand still
Like time
Our watches are broken
But we wind them anyway

We realize
The error in our ways
By the straightening of tree branches
Reaching up
To the sky
To touch the face of God

Like antennae
Guiding in satellites from space
The expressions of angels
Contemptuous

It is easy to fit in
Like a cog in a wheel
Turning circles

These ghostly machines
Grinding to a halt
Fading

These memories are apparitions
Intelligence of their how/when/why
Falling back from stormy skies
Coming down off of sixties-era highs

Reverberating Jesus
Moms and dads and country vacations
Ice cream cones
Looking out over mountains

To take a deep breath of twilight fog
Settling for coffee

Now
That is freedom

Sometimes when our blood
Boils through pores onto the linoleum
Of bathrooms decorated with butterflies

Sometimes when we posture
For the camera
Our sex exploding
Upon command of darkness

Sometimes when we write
Our books become failed exploits
Of conquered skin
Of planting flags

Sometimes when we are devastated
At what we have done

We realize that you can see right through us
The honesty of a look
We realize that you can see right through us
Our 80s concert tees
Our fetal position raptures
Our messianic puberty
Thumb sucking

Sometimes when it happens
          It happens
Sometimes when it happens
          It happens

Sometimes
We just wanna know
That we didn't screw up

Big Bang

Carpet remnants
Decorate the closet wooden floor

I am moved to wonder:

If Michelangelo were alive,
Would he paint my ceiling?

Gridlock

A refusal to drive any longer
Put the gear shift into park
Switch the clothing into hiking gear
I fear that I will be a few moments late
I ask that a few cents be taken off of my first hour

Thursday Morning Last-Minute Love Poem

Last night
I imagined you
Hiding behind wedding dresses

Your hand
Extending like always

I volunteer information
To people

That love is love is...
To steal from a song

Perhaps my originality has become stale

Yet
My lips quiver
Leaving my heart to flutter
As you kiss me

And I have never shared this
With you
Because as much
As I want to share everything with you
There are a few things
I'd like to keep to myself
Like my bad moments
Like my coy smiles

I apologize

Last night
I imagined you
Hiding behind wedding dresses

I mentally photographed
Autumn trees

Dancing

Their leaves falling
Kamikaze
To crunch beneath my feet

Love is a constant
A chase
To make this poem original

Perhaps my complexities
Are not so complex at all

But I love you
And the sun setting is not enough
To settle my soul when you are
Simply across a vast space
A living room
From me

I long for your touch
Your coy smiles

I love you
Thankfully

Last night
I imagined you
Hiding behind wedding dresses

I performed this poem
As it hollowed out
My grey matter

Proving me unbound
For you complete me
As a soulmate could

As life gets a little too

Crazy
I am crazy about you
We are joined through heartbeats

These are thoughts
That sculpt the acmes of mountains
Out of thinner air
Than an exhalation of a final breath

Those acmes
Remind me that I am never alone

I love you

Illinois!

I'm a guitar-crazy charcoal-faced teenager!

I'm thinking about Boston
Irish Cream Lattes and stealing snack cakes
From the corner store

I could've been a Southie
With curly Q greased out hair
But I'm in Illinois

Jessica is wandering through my room
Trying to collect her clothes
Her bra
Panties crumpled up just underneath my denim blues
Holes in the knees
Worn out from climbing too many trees
Their leaves/green
Ready to die a little too soon
Like the rest of us teenagers living here
Sick of living here
Nothing ever happens here
Except last year (you remember?)
When those guys got drunk
Drove their pickup into the light pole
Outside of the fast food joint
McSomething's

We were all there to see it
Since McSomething's is the only place
To hang out at
To have a sing along at

I don't care how we got this far in Illinois!

I'm dreaming of ancient Roman ruins
How they crumble at my touch

Where my name is Jupiter at best
With curly Q greased out hair
But I'm in Illinois

No
I'm in Boca Raton
I'm in the nearest bar
I'm in your head
I'm in Illinois

And I'm guitar-crazy!

The way Jessica goes crazy
When I go out for a beer
Stolen from my old man
From the refrigerator in the garage
Next to the '77 Nova with the endless oil leak
Next to the stench of the burned out engine

The way Jessica goes crazy
Trying to find a polite way
To say that she is bored
With another night of fantasizing
About anywhere but here

Where in the Effingham are we?
Slipped from my tongue
Into her cheeks

Guitar-crazy!

The way she is
Complacent about growing old here
A place just like anywhere else
But without the only game in town

A place just like anywhere else
Full of victims and no crime
If only we had an all night diner
We could sleep it off over breakfast at 3 a.m.

Oh, Illinois!

Taking Sides

Sometimes
I wish I could assume a different name
New clothes
Tossing off these old tattered rags
Letting the sparrows come in
To build a nest out of me
While I'm texting my new friends
Looking to pay my way through this life
To go to the mountain

Sometimes
I wish I could dance and bring the rain
To wash away everything
That would be considered overtly dark
In this rocking back and forth of my body
In the corner of a pitch black room
When there is nothing as scary as childhood
Where learning to ride a bike
Is more of a success in life
Than landing a six-figure-a-year job

This is the day where planes aren't allowed to fly
Where we are not allowed to speak our minds aloud

This is the day where the pains of life are less a pain
Than the constant circling of our bodies to make a bed

Where we will nestle down for a rest
While the rest of the world travels like ants to home and work

Where we will sing operatic systematic rhythmic slacking
Where we will hitch the trailer to the truck and go camping

Where we will become one with nature and kill a ten point buck
Where I wish we could dream like real geniuses

Where we will embrace mathematics to solve the equation of

Love plus lust equals/this is the day where my scars will shine

Where the stars are just as arrogant to think that our worship
Is for the stars/are just as arrogant to think that it's all about them

Where I know this/where I am awesome/where I am a star
Where I will sit on my back porch/guiding the ships
Into port/letting them dock/letting them trade their lives for

A slow motion fly through the air
Heads
Tails
Which way will it land?

I'm perfect underneath this bridge over troubled like a stolen lyric

All of the best thieves steal (I'm just waiting for a ride)
Scrambled eggs and sausage (can you loan me a dollar?)

I stand like the Rock of Gibraltar
I bite like a white shark
I touch like an abandoned building
I love like the widening crevice of an earthquake
I think like a statue
I laugh like an ordinary guy
I remember like a photograph
I eat like an anorexic
I have taken the final sip from the coffee

Addictions
From bones
From lips
From gambling
Red number
Pays the loser
Water cooler
Conversation
Did you?
Did she?

Something awkward mumbled as they walk away

Confused by the television
Rock bottom prices and Crazy Larry
This is the last time/I tell ya/the last time
That we are taking something literally

Bones

This is supposed to be artistic expression
Piling up the wadded pieces of paper
Bleaching the words out of them
Hanging them out to dry in the summer afternoon

I'm going home
Taking my toys with me

I have something on my mind
More than bone
Juicy fluids
Naturally curly hair

I'm going home
With Ahab on my mind

I could keep floating
When I land
I probably will

The photographs of loved ones
Creased inside of the palm of my hand
Scarred

I warned my family
To be suspicious of everything
Everyone

I warned my family
To be suspicious of unattended bags
In public areas

I warned them to leave
Just leave
Don't stay there

I am practicing what I preach

This is post 9/11 America
This is not what God wants

This is supposed to be artistic expression
Piling up the wadded pieces of paper
Bleaching the words out of them
Hanging them out to dry in the summer afternoon

I am closing this chapter of my life
Time to start over

No Life in Trade for Freedom

I met a little boy
His trigger finger was quicker
Than he could jump
To slam dunk on a giant
Towering over his little brown body

Super tanned in the African sunshine

Traded off for revolution
Against a warlord
His face
Striped
From the bars that are
Non-existent
But real just the same
When it comes to growing up
Normally

Anti-normalcy
Sprinkled as salt
Over
Wounds
Freshly seared meat
Hanging over a spit

A fire burning
The world turning
An axis of assholes

They say that no life is worth the price of freedom
I say that life is the nucleus of freedom

Met a little girl
Her face
Soft like her mama's face

She played with dolls in her room

Away from the violence of the city
No seventies sitcom innocence

Epstein's mother wrote a suicide note
This week
To present to the class

She has a love for art
For hogs sweating in the summer heat

The streetlights hiss
The end of the day
The beginning of the party
The wake

The hearty hunger to be fulfilled
By the theft of choice

She had no chance
They say
Except to turn tricks to
Get food onto her table
To get a package when
She was aching
When she was jonesing

They say that tomorrow isn't written in the stars
I say that tomorrow is the memory of a gut instinct

Met an awestruck mother
Her baby graduating from college
The first of the family to succeed
To spite the teardrops
That saturated the table cloth
Late at night
With war on the TV

Baby mama
Baby daddy

Fighting over who the father is

Maury Povich
Is
Jerry Springer
Is
Whitney
Is
Bobby
Is
Domestic Violence riddled childhoods

Would you hit your lady
Hit your man
Hit your kids
Would you!?!?!
Would you!?!?!

I have seen the future
And it will be the Songs of Solomon
At the top of the charts

They say that real history is ripped from the headlines
I say that real history is written in the footsteps we choose to follow

Smiles

Within our smiles

Tempestuous springtime flowers bloom wildly
Our arms stretched
Pythonesque
Constriction

We don't mind
Eternally
Twenty-nine years and miles travelled
To meet for a cup of coffee

Within our smiles

Reflections of two lovers kissing
Over a simple stream
In our pasts
A city of lights
Exalting the electricity
In between

To concede defeat
As we have won each other
Over a quiet hello

Over dinner
Over well-planned drink festivities
Asking for hands
In lieu of opuses scrawled onto napkins
Turning beautiful notes into sweet harmony
Turning sentimental journeys into poetic philosophy
And jazz fusion sound

Within our smiles

We play for our children
As they grow older
To find their own loves
To lose those loves
To find them once more
Secure in the way that our hands
Were brought together by God

Jack Kerouac Post Script

And I'll say it again

Your poetry sucked, Jack
But I respected it

Just like I respect your suicide slow
Motion measure that failed when it was
Posed to Congress in '69

Mexican sands were blowing
Neckties were flipping in the breeze
So beautiful
Childish
Simple
Columbian
Fraternity
Over drinks and literary talk
Beneath dust jackets stapled to the wall

You gave us a tantrum
And we threw ourselves onto the ground
As if we were the ones who were suffering

Man/you were building a movement
Out of prostitutes and mile-long stretches
Of dirty roads/desolate/ethereal/perfect

But your poetry sucked, Jack
Dying before you realized your true potential

And we love you for it

The Winning Touchdown

Late night
Friday night
Under the lights
I'm uptight
Pacing the sidelines
Looking for an honesty
In why I'm here

Remembering what was told to me
It's only a game
But if I drop the ball
Heads will hang in shame

Pardon me, sir
I'm looking for the model life
Easy street
Living for what is right
And
What is right is honesty

Daydreaming of camouflage
Jones is going in
Lining up on the far left
Digs his cleats in
To the fresh autumn mud

These are the longest seconds
Of life

I can hear my family
Echoes of pride
Burrowing into my brain

I practice restraint
The crowd falls to a hush

Down
Set
Hike

The Blues

John Lennon said it best
That he was lonely
But it was Miles who put it mildly
When disputing what love is to be free
To be a missing person on a milk carton
Is to be the blues

Walking with a swagger
This is the music that mastered
The identity of the saxophone
The contradiction of a piano
A happiness in being sad
Is to be the blues

I'm sick of myself
Writing about solids
No gases to come and dazzle my eyes
Tickle my brain stem into seeing visions
Of holy Ginsberg references

But poetry notwithstanding
But outstanding
All eyes are on the world
The emotional ties that lump us together
As sensitive human beings
All fifteen thousandths of a percent of us

We are not your typical soul
Jive
Love lumber
Cutting down trees to build a memory
We are not your catalysts
To destroy entire cultures

We are ten minutes of a song
To monitor your heart rate
To demonize your rationale

To become the blues

John Lennon said it best
That he was lonely
But it was Miles who put it mildly
When disputing love is to be free
To be a missing person on a milk carton
Is to be the blues

This is what it is to be the blues

But what do you do
When the music stops?